Published in 1990 by A&C Black (Publishers) Limited
35 Bedford Row, London WC1R 4JH, England

ISBN 0-382-39758-4 (LSB) 1 2 3 4 5 6 7 8 9 10
ISBN 0-382-39763-0 (pbk) 1 2 3 4 5 6 7 8 9 10

First published in 1998 in the United States by Silver Burdett Press

A Division of Simon & Schuster
299 Jefferson Road, Parsippany, NJ 07054

Library of Congress Cataloging-in-Publication Data
Coldrey, Jennifer
Mosquito/by Jennifer Coldrey and George Bernard.
p.   cm. (Stopwatch series)
Originally published: London, England: A&C Black, © 1990.
Includes index.
Summary: In photographs and brief text, examines the life cycle of the mosquito.
1. Mosquitoes—Juvenile literature. 2. Mosquitoes—Life cycles—Juvenile literature.
[1. Mosquitoes.] I. Bernard, George, 1949–   . II. Title. III. Series.
QL536.C55   1997   96-22648
595.77′1—dc20   CIP   AC

Acknowledgments
The Illustrations are by Helen Senior

The publisher would like to thank Michael Chinery for his help and advice.

Filmset by August Filmsetting, Haydock, St Helens
Colour reproduction by Hong Kong Graphic Arts Ltd
Printed in Belgium by Proost Interntional Bookproduction

Mosquito

Jennifer Coldrey
Photographs by George Bernard

Silver Burdett Press
Parsippany, New Jersey

Here is a mosquito.

Have you ever been bitten by a mosquito? You can find mosquitoes in summer, near ponds and ditches.

Look at the big picture. This mosquito is drinking sweet juice from a flower. It sucks up the juice through a long, sharp tube sticking out from its mouth. The female mosquito uses this tube to suck blood.

This book will tell you about the life of a mosquito.

The mosquito finds a mate.

Look at the big photograph. This male mosquito is on a leaf. Can you see the bushy antennae sticking out of his head? They look a lot like brushes.

Mosquitoes use their antennae for touching and smelling. The male mosquito uses his antennae to find a mate. He knows when he has found a female because of the humming noise she makes with her wings. He flies toward her and they mate.

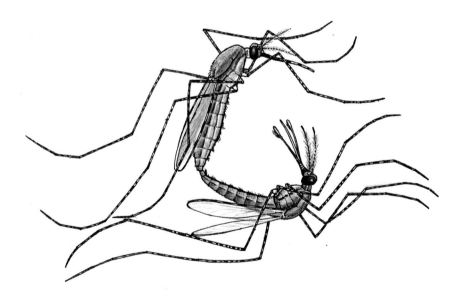

After she has mated, the female flies off to find food.

The female mosquito sucks blood.

The female mosquito needs to drink blood to make her eggs grow inside her. This mosquito has landed on a man's hand. First she feels around with her mouth. Then she pricks the skin with a needle-sharp tube called a proboscis.

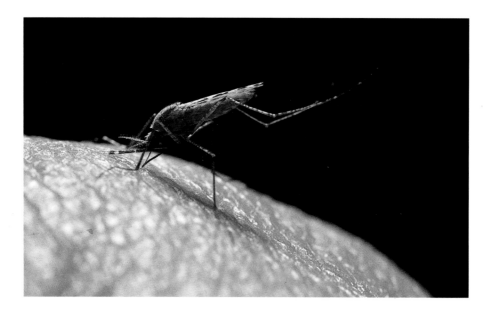

She uses her proboscis to suck out the blood.

Look at the big photograph. Can you see the blood inside the mosquito's body? Before she flies away, she leaves a drop of blood behind.

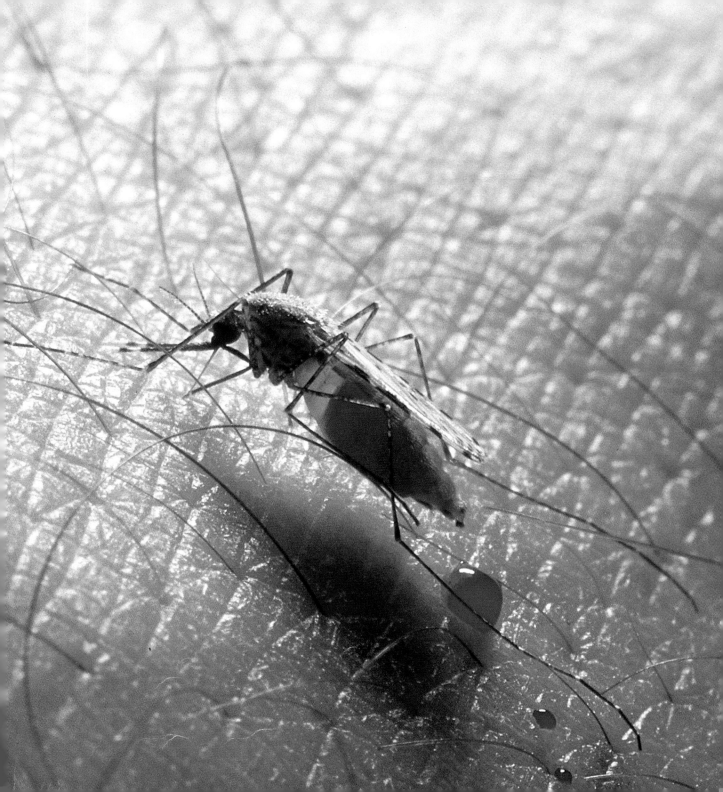

The mosquito lays her eggs.

The female mosquito finds a pool of water. She lays her eggs one by one into the water.

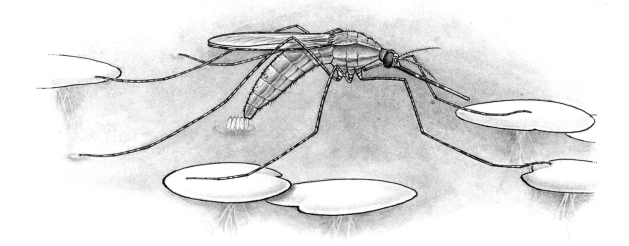

Then she will fly away.

The eggs float together in groups on top of the water. Each egg looks like a tiny boat. In the photograph the eggs look very big. In real life they are small. Each one is as big as the top of a needle. Can you see the air bubbles on each side of every egg? These bubbles keep the eggs from sinking.

The eggs hatch.

After a few days tiny creatures hatch out of the eggs. They are mosquito larvae. They float at the top of the water.

Look at the big photograph. Can you see the bristles sticking out from the sides of the larvae? These bristles help to keep the larvae afloat.

This drawing shows a larva close up.

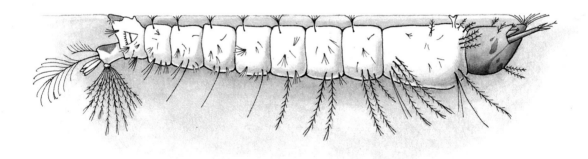

Its body is divided into segments. It moves by bending and wriggling its body.

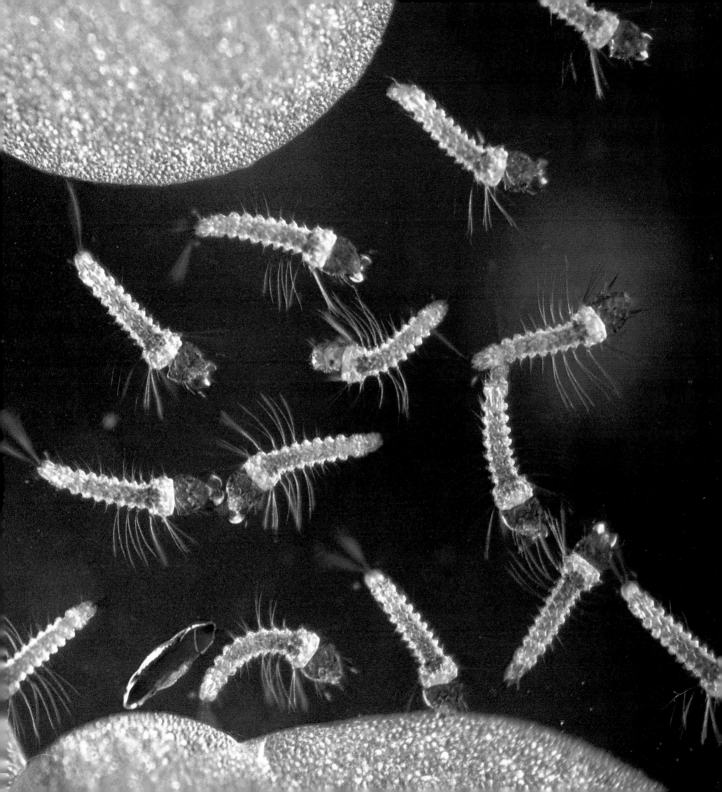

The larva grows bigger.

The larva eats tiny plants and animals it finds in the water. It catches the food with special hairy brushes that stick out from its head. Then it sweeps the food into its mouth.

As the larva grows bigger, its skin gets too tight. Then the larva's skin splits open. This larva is wriggling out of its skin.

It has grown a new skin underneath. The larva will change its skin four times before it is fully grown.

The larva changes into a pupa.

This mosquito larva is about ten days old.

It has grown very fat. Its body is a creamy color. Soon it will change its skin for the last time.

Look at the big photograph. The larva's skin has split open, and a pupa has come out.

The new pupa is very pale. Its body curves around like a comma. Can you see its dark eyes?

Inside the pupa the larva is changing.

The pupa has no mouth and does not eat. It usually floats at the top of the water. But it can dive down to escape from danger. It has paddles on the end of its tail to help it swim.

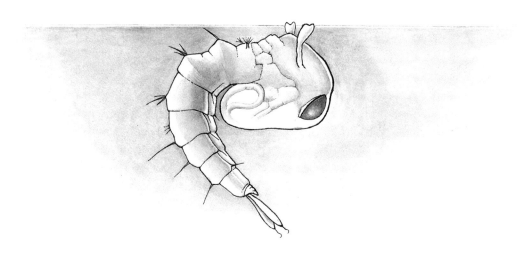

Can you see two tubes sticking out from the back of the pupa?

The tubes poke through the water and take in air so that the pupa can breathe.

As the pupa gets older, it becomes darker in color. Inside, the pupa is turning into an adult mosquito.

The pupa changes into an adult mosquito.

Look at the big photograph. This pupa is six days old.
The mosquito has finished growing inside the pupa.
Now it is ready to come out from the pupal skin.
The pupa stretches out along the top of the water.
Then it pushes its back up out of the water.

The skin of the pupa starts to split. First the mosquito
pushes its head out.

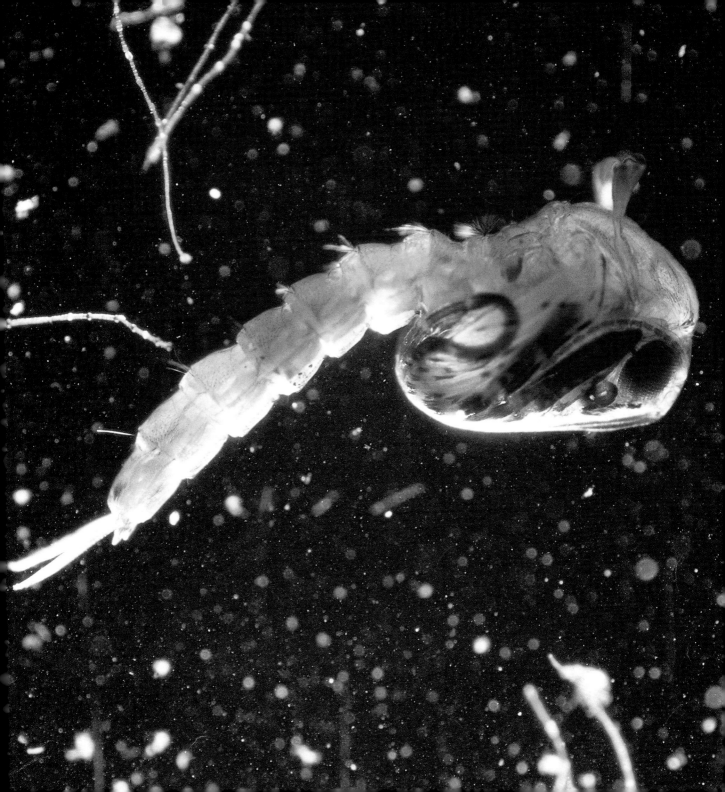

The adult mosquito appears.

The mosquito pushes itself up out of the water.

It wriggles the front end of its body out of the old skin.

Look at the big photograph. The mosquito has pulled its wings free. Now it is pulling its legs out. The mosquito takes less than ten minutes to struggle out of the pupal skin.

The adult mosquito rests on the water.

This mosquito is nearly out of the pupal skin.

The mosquito is a female. Her body is soft and swollen. She cannot fly yet. She rests on the water.

Look at the big photograph. The mosquito's wings are now stiff and dry. Her legs are firm and strong. After about five minutes she will fly away to find food. Soon she will mate.

What do you think will happen then?

Do you remember how the mosquito came from an egg?
See if you can tell the story in your own words.
You can use these pictures to help you.

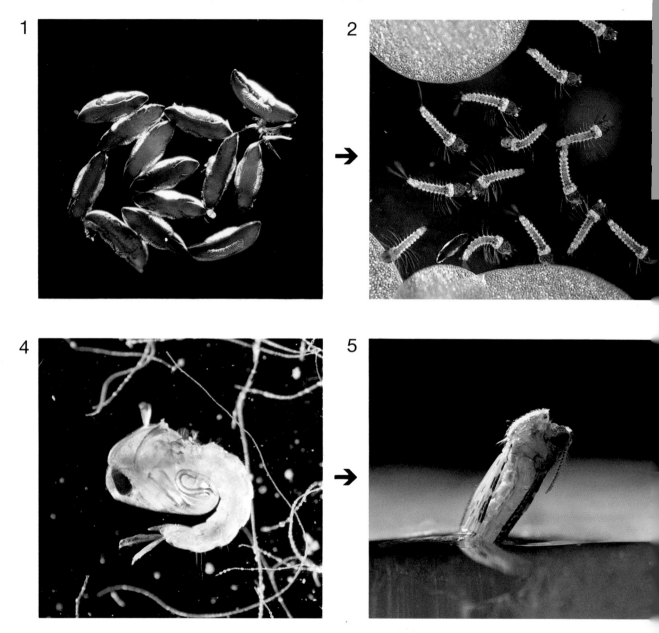

1

2

4

5

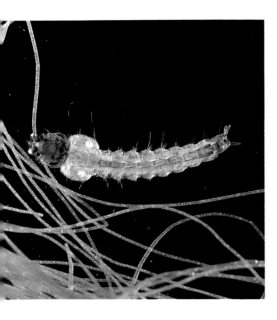

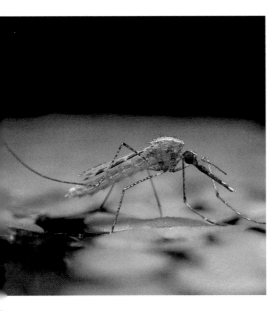

Index

This index will help you to find some of the important words in this book.

When you visit a pond, look out for mosquitoes flying over the water. Can you see larvae and pupae in the water?